My Pet Hamster

BY ANNE ROCKWELL

ILLUSTRATED BY BERNICE LUM

HarperCollins*Publishers*

For Henry, Caesar, Basil, Daisy, James, Monkey,
and Big Daisy
—A.R.

For Miss Eva
—B.L.

Special thanks to Martha McDonnell
and the staff of Animal Kind Veterinary Hospital
for their time and expert review

The *Let's-Read-and-Find-Out Science* book series was originated by Dr. Franklyn M. Branley, Astronomer Emeritus and former Chairman of the American Museum–Hayden Planetarium, and was formerly co-edited by him and Dr. Roma Gans, Professor Emeritus of Childhood Education, Teachers College, Columbia University. Text and illustrations for each of the books in the series are checked for accuracy by an expert in the relevant field. For more information about Let's-Read-and-Find-Out Science books, write to HarperCollins Children's Books, 1350 Avenue of the Americas, New York, NY 10019, or visit our website at www.letsreadandfindout.com.

HarperCollins®, ♣®, and Let's Read-and-Find-Out Science® are trademarks of HarperCollins Publishers Inc.
My Pet Hamster
Text copyright © 2002 by Anne Rockwell
Illustrations copyright © 2002 by Bernice Lum
Printed in the U.S.A. All rights reserved.

Library of Congress Cataloging-in-Publication Data
Rockwell, Anne F.
My pet hamster / by Anne Rockwell ; illustrated by Bernice Lum.
p.   cm. — (Let's-read-and-find-out science. Stage 1)
Summary: Describes what pet hamsters are like, what they eat, and how they act, and explains the difference between wild and domestic animals.
ISBN 0-06-028564-8 — ISBN 0-06-445205-0 (pbk.) — ISBN 0-06-028565-6 (lib. bdg.)
1. Hamsters as pets—Juvenile literature. [1. Hamsters.   2. Pets.]   I. Lum, Bernice, ill.   II. Title.   III. Series.
SF459.H3 R63   2002   2001026481   636.9'356—dc21

1 2 3 4 5 6 7 8 9 10   ❖   First Edition

My Pet Hamster

My hamster lives in a shiny wire cage on the bookcase in my room.

5

My hamster was my birthday present. I picked it out at the pet store. Its mother had ten baby hamsters. I counted them. I couldn't decide which one I liked best. But when mine crawled over to me, I knew it was the one I wanted. The salesperson said it was one month old.

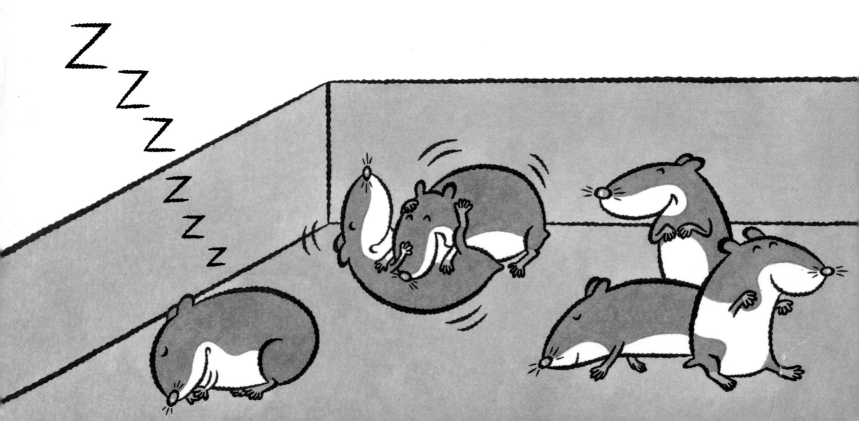

We bought a wire cage with a feeding dish, a water bottle, a bag of wood shavings, and a box of special hamster food.

My hamster is four months old now, but it's already as big as it will ever get. My little cousin Caroline is six months old, but she's still a baby.

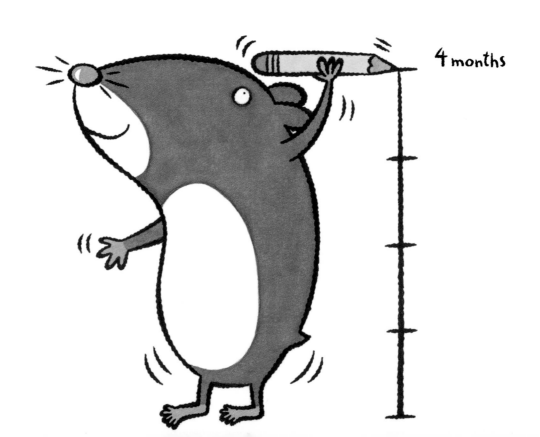

4 months

6 months

Hamsters finish growing
sooner than people do.

11

12

When I take my pet hamster out of the cage, I like to feel its tiny, smooth, pink feet. I like to touch its cool, pink nose. I look into its round, black eyes and it looks back at me. Its whiskers twitch.

Some hamsters have
long, fluffy fur,

and some have short fur,
but all have pink noses
and pink feet.

14

Mine is called a golden
hamster, because it has
golden fur.

A hamster is a kind of animal called a rodent.
All rodents have large front teeth called incisors,
soft fur, round eyes, and whiskers.

Mice, rabbits, squirrels, chipmunks, rats, guinea pigs, and gerbils are rodents, too.

Every day I feed my hamster. It needs the hard food we get at the pet store to gnaw on with its sharp front teeth. If it didn't have hard food, those teeth would grow, and grow, and grow. My teeth and yours don't grow longer and longer, but rodent teeth do.

My hamster always eats its regular food, but sometimes I give it a tiny piece of parsley or carrot for a treat. But I never give it candy. That would make it sick. Every morning I fill up the bottle that hangs on the cage so that my hamster always has fresh water to drink.

22

Every Saturday I clean my hamster's cage. That's a big job, so my father helps. I put my hamster in a cardboard box while we clean its cage. But I don't ever need to brush or wash my hamster. It can clean itself. It puts one pink paw in its mouth, then scratches its fur or rubs its paw across its face. That's how my hamster washes its fur.

24

Hamsters need to run and play and get exercise, just like me. Mine has a wheel in its cage to run around and around on. It likes to make the wheel turn faster and faster. It also has a cardboard tube that used to hold paper towels. It runs through this dark tunnel and comes out the other end.

At night, when I go to bed, I sometimes hear my hamster running on his wheel and through his cardboard tube. That's because wild hamsters are nocturnal animals—they stay awake at night. Sometimes my hamster is so noisy that I put his cage on the bookcase in the hall so he won't keep me awake.

There are many different kinds of animals in our world. Some are wild and some are tame. Wild animals find their own food and places to live, but human beings take care of tame animals. We also call them domestic animals. They need us and we need them. Cows give us milk.

Chickens lay eggs.

Sheep give us wool.
We give these
animals fields and
barns where they
can eat and sleep.

Pets are tame animals that live with us. They keep us company and play with us. My grandmother has a canary that lives in a golden cage and sings. My friend Jack has a frog that lives in a glass aquarium.

Our neighbors have a cat that comes to visit me, and my teacher has a new puppy.

We take care of our pets, and our pets keep us company and make us happy.
We don't give wild animals names.
But we always give our pets names.
My hamster's name is Silky.

- Try to name as many domestic animals as you can. Make a list. Next to each animal's name, put down how it helps people.

- Wild hamsters live in the Middle East and Asia, from Syria to Siberia. The golden hamsters that people keep as pets are all descended from one group of wild hamsters that were caught in Syria in 1930. Sometimes they are called Syrian hamsters. Look at a map or a globe. Can you find the part of the world that wild hamsters come from?

- Make a list of all the animals you saw today. How many are wild? How many are domestic? How many are pets?

- Do you have a pet? Does it live in a cage or an aquarium, or does it sleep on a cushion in your house? What is its name? Can you draw a picture of it?

33

JP   Rockwell, Anne F.

My pet hamster.